Exploring Shapes™

Circles and Spheres

Bonnie Coulter Leech

The Rosen Publishing Group's
PowerKids Press™
New York

To Bill and Billy—the wind beneath my wings

Published in 2007 by The Rosen Publishing Group, Inc.
29 East 21st Street, New York, NY 10010

First Edition

Editors: Daryl Heller and Kara Murray
Book Design: Elana Davidian

Photo Credits: Cover © Philip James Corwin/Corbis; p. 4 © Michael Cogliantry/Getty Images; p. 5 © White Cross Production/Getty Images; p. 7 © Maps.com/IndexStock Imagery, Inc; p. 10 © age fotostock/SuperStock; p. 11 © Royalty-Free/Corbis; p. 15 © Inga Spence/IndexStock Imagery, Inc; p. 16 Erich Lessing/Art Resource, NY; p. 17 © Bettmann/Corbis; p. 19 © Kevin Schafer/zefa/Corbis; p. 20 © Kindra Clineff/IndexStock Imagery, Inc; p. 21 © Bill Losh/Getty Images.

Library of Congress Cataloging-in-Publication Data

Leech, Bonnie Coulter.
   Circles and spheres / Bonnie Coulter Leech.— 1st ed.
       p. cm. — (Exploring shapes)
   Includes bibliographical references and index.
   ISBN 1-4042-3494-2 (lib. bdg.)
   1. Circle—Juvenile literature. 2. Sphere—Juvenile literature. I. Title. II. Series.
   QA484.L395 2007
   516'.152—dc22

                                2005028072

Manufactured in the United States of America

Contents

1	Circles	4
2	Point, Line, and Plane	6
3	What Is a Circle?	8
4	Radius	10
5	Chords and Diameter	12
6	Circumference	14
7	Pi	16
8	Symmetry	18
9	Spheres	20
10	The Family of Circles and Spheres	22
	Glossary	23
	Index	24
	Web Sites	24

Circles

Have you ever noticed how many objects are round? There are many things around us that have round shapes. Round shapes are known as circles. Many clocks are round. The numbers on a clock face are laid out in a circle. As the hands of a clock move, they also form a circle. Look at a dinner plate. Many dinner plates are also in the shape of circles.

These coins are in the shape of circles. They are some of the many round things you might see every day. How many other round objects can you think of that you see every day?

What about the glass that holds your milk? The top of a drinking glass is usually round. Trace your finger around the top of the glass. As your finger goes around the top of the glass, you are making a circle. The top of a glass **represents** a circle.

Take a look at a quarter, a dime, or a nickel. These coins are made in the shape of a circle. Look at the wheels of a bicycle. The wheels of a bicycle are also round. Bicycle wheels are made in the shape of circles.

What makes a round shape a circle? What are the parts of a circle? Let's find out.

This girl is playing with a hula hoop. A hula hoop is a toy that is in the shape of a circle. Another toy that is shaped like a circle is a Frisbee.

Mathematicians often use certain terms that can be used to describe circles and other shapes. Some of these terms are "point," "line," and "plane."

A point has no **dimensions**. It does not have length, width, or thickness. A point is represented by a dot (•). A point is named using a capital letter, such as point A.

A line has only one dimension. That dimension is length. A line is a set of points in a straight path that has no beginning and no end (⟷). A line is named using two points on the line, such as line *AB*.

A   B

A plane is a flat surface, like a flat sheet of paper. However, a plane in geometry is **infinitely** wide and infinitely long. A plane has no thickness. All **two-dimensional** shapes, like circles, exist in a plane.

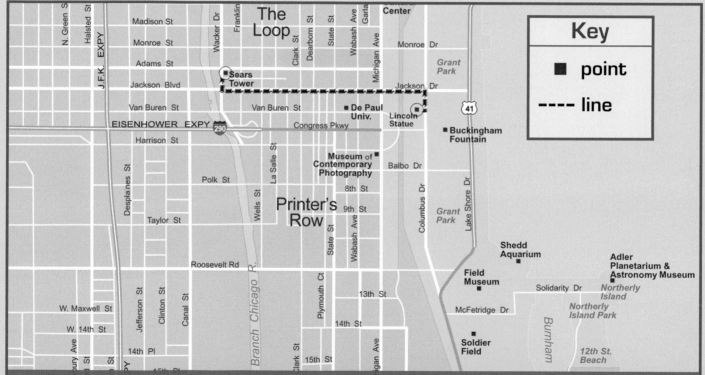

The lines on a map show roads and where they lead. The points on a map show places. The lines drawn on this map show the roads that lead from the Lincoln Statue, one point on this map, to the Sears Tower, another point on this map.

What Is a Circle?

Suppose a farmer ties a horse to a long rope that is connected to a pole. With no trees or other **obstacles** to get in the way, the horse can move around the pole at the full length of the rope. The path formed as the horse walks around is in the shape of a circle. Every point on the path is formed using the same length of the rope.

Circles are flat, two-dimensional figures. A circle is the **set** of all points in a plane that are the same **distance** from a given point.

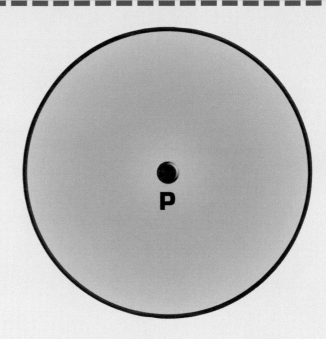

This is circle P.

That point is called the center of the circle. In the example below, the pole is the center of the circle. Circles are named using the point at the center of the circle.

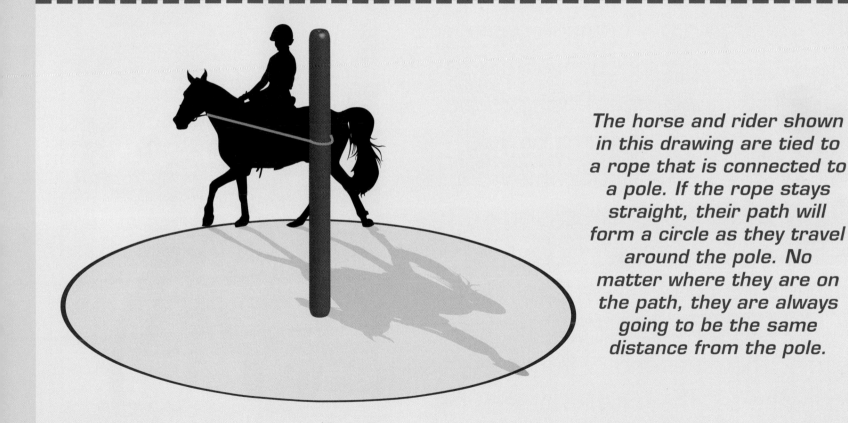

The horse and rider shown in this drawing are tied to a rope that is connected to a pole. If the rope stays straight, their path will form a circle as they travel around the pole. No matter where they are on the path, they are always going to be the same distance from the pole.

A circle's radius is any line segment that you can draw from the center of the circle to a point on the circle. A circle has many radii. Radii are more than one radius. Picture a bicycle wheel. The spokes that come from the center of the wheel are all radii.

Picture the roped horse walking around the path. One end of the rope is tied to the pole, or the center of the circle. The other end of the rope is tied to the horse. The rope represents the radius of the path formed by the horse.

The spokes that come from the center of bicycle wheels are all radii.

A radius is a line segment. A line segment is part of a line with two endpoints. The radius of a circle has one endpoint at the center of the circle. The other endpoint of the radius is a point that lies on the circle.

As the horse moves around the circle, the rope's length doesn't change. At every point on the circle, there is a radius. All radii of a circle are the same length.

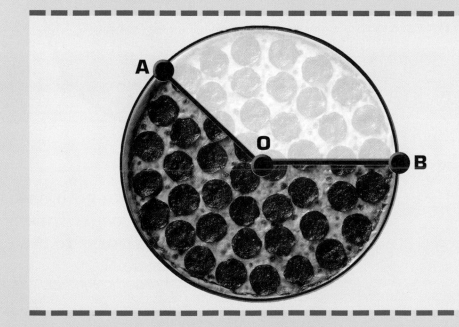

A radius is named using two endpoints of a line segment. In circle O radius OA is the same length as radius OB.

A line segment that connects two points on a circle is called a chord. The endpoints of a chord lie on the circle. The length of a chord depends on where on the circle it lies. The closer a chord is to the center of a circle, the longer the chord is. The farther away the chord is from the center of the circle, the shorter the chord is. Can you look at a circle and see why? Where would the longest chord of a circle be?

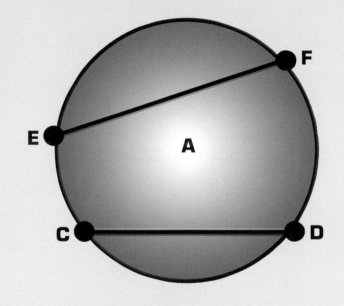

Chord *CD* and chord *EF* are both part of circle *A*. chord *EF* is longer than chord *CD* because it is closer to the center of Circle *A*.

A chord that passes through the center of the circle is the longest chord of the circle. That chord has a special name. It is called the diameter. The diameter goes through the center of the circle and **divides** the circle into two equal parts. Each half of a divided circle is called a semicircle.

In circle C, shown here, the diameter *MN* passes through the center. A radius is a line segment that connects the center of the circle to a point on the circle. The diameter of a circle is made of two radii. Diameter *MN* is made up of two radii, radius *CM* and radius *CN*. The diameter of a circle is twice the length of its radius.

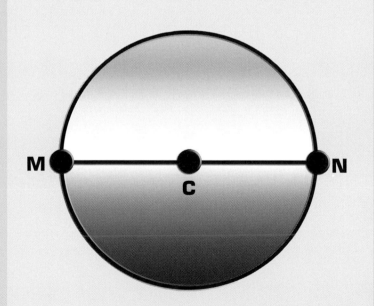

Circumference

The distance around any **geometric** shape is called the perimeter. You can trace the perimeter with your finger by going around the outside of the geometric figure.

The perimeter around a circle has a special name. It is called the circumference. The path that the horse makes as it walks around the pole represents the circumference of the path.

If you trace your finger around a circular object, you are tracing the circumference. Let's experiment. Find several objects that have a circular shape. You might use a trash can with a round top, or a paper plate. Use a piece of string to measure the distance around your object. Straighten the string and measure the length on a ruler. This length represents the circumference, or the distance around the circle.

The man shown here is measuring the distance around this tree. Since the distance around the tree is a circle, he is measuring the circumference.

Mathematicians have discovered many things about circles. If you measure a circle, you will make some discoveries about circles, too. Measure the circumference of a circle. Then measure the length of the diameter of the same circle. You will discover that the circumference is a little more than three times longer than the diameter.

If the measurements are done again using circles of

The ancient Egyptians were very skilled mathematicians. They applied their knowledge of geometry to building and making art. This gold plate was a gift from an Egyptian ruler to a general in the Egyptian army.

different sizes, you will find that the circumference is always a little more than three times longer than the diameter. This type of comparison is called a ratio. A ratio can be written like a **fraction**. The ratio of the circumference (C) to the diameter (d) can be represented by the fraction C/d and will always be the same number. This number is called pi. Pi is a very long number, but it is about equal to 3.1416. The **symbol** for pi is π.

Euclid (above) was a Greek mathematician who lived in the third century B.C. He wrote a book of geometry called *Elements*.

Symmetry

Have you ever noticed that many shapes, including circles, can be folded in such a way that the two sides of the shape match exactly? Look at the letter H, for example. The letter H can be folded so that one side matches the other. In fact you can fold the letter H two ways so that the parts match each other.

Circles are symmetrical. This means that one half of a circle looks like the other half of a circle. When you fold a circle over its diameter, the two sides fit together exactly. The diameter, or fold line, is called the line of symmetry. The line of symmetry is the imaginary line that divides a shape in half.

Some geometric shapes have only one line of symmetry. Look at the letter T. The letter T can be folded only one way so that the sides match exactly. Other geometric shapes have many lines of symmetry. The letter H, a rectangle, and a square all have many lines of symmetry. Because a circle has many diameters, it can be folded many different ways. Each time it is folded, a circle has symmetry. Therefore, a circle has many lines of symmetry.

Many things in nature have symmetry. If you drew a line down the middle of the butterfly shown here, you would see that both halves have the exact same shape.

Spheres

A sphere is a solid figure that is shaped like a ball. A sphere has a smooth, curved surface. Every point on a sphere is the same distance from the sphere's center, as in a circle. A sphere also has a center point and many radii, just as a circle does. However, spheres are **three-dimensional**. A two-dimensional circle has only length and width. A sphere, which is three-dimensional, has not only length and width but also thickness.

The dotted line on this globe represents the equator. The Northern Hemisphere is the top half of the globe, and the Southern Hemisphere is the bottom half.

Spheres play an important part in everyday life. Spheres are the shapes that are used to make baseballs, basketballs, and globes.

Many games are played with spheres. Think about how hard it would be to play basketball or baseball if the balls were not shaped like spheres!

Earth is almost in the shape of a sphere. It is often represented by a globe that is in the shape of a sphere. Earth is divided in half by the equator. The equator divides Earth into two equal hemispheres. A hemisphere is half of a sphere. North America is said to be located in the Northern Hemisphere of Earth.

The Family of Circles and Spheres

Circles and spheres are important in everyday life. How useful would a wheel be if it were not shaped like a circle? Imagine how bumpy the ride on a wagon would be if wheels were not in the shape of circles. Wheels that are circles give a smooth ride because every point on the wheel is the same distance from the center of the wheel.

Imagine how hard it would be to play basketball with a ball that was shaped like a triangle. With basketballs shaped like spheres, it is much easier to play basketball. The basketball **hoop**, too, is shaped like a circle. Its shape makes it easier for a sphere to fit inside the hoop. These are just a few of the many wonderful uses of circles and spheres!

Glossary

dimensions (duh-MEN-shunz) The length, width, or height of an object.

distance (DIS-tens) The length between two points.

divides (dih-VYDZ) Breaks apart or separates.

fraction (FRAK-shun) A number that stands for part of a whole.

geometric (jee-uh-MEH-trik) Having to do with a type of math that deals with straight lines, circles, and other shapes.

hoop (HOOP) A round object that is shaped like a ring.

infinitely (IN-feh-net-lee) Having no end.

mathematicians (math-muh-TIH-shunz) People who study numbers.

obstacles (OB-stih-kulz) Things that are in the way.

represents (reh-prih-ZENTS) Stands for.

set (SET) A group of numbers, objects, or things.

symbol (SIM-bul) An object or a picture that stands for something else.

three-dimensional (three-deh-MENCH-nul) Having height, width, and depth.

two-dimensional (too-deh-MENCH-nul) Able to be measured two ways, by length and by width.

Index

C
center of the circle, 9–10, 12–13
chord, 12
circumference, 14, 16–17

D
diameter, 12–13, 16–19
dimensions, 6

G
geometry, 7

H
hemisphere, 21

L
length, 6, 8, 11–14, 16
line(s), 6
line segment, 11–12

P
perimeter, 14
pi, 16–17
plane, 6–7

point(s), 6, 8–9

R
radius, 10, 13
ratio, 17

S
semicircle, 13
set, 8
sphere, 20
symmetry, 18–19

Web Sites

Due to the changing nature of Internet links, PowerKids Press has developed an online list of Web sites related to the subject of this book. This site is updated regularly. Please use this link to access the list:
www.powerkidslinks.com/psgs/circles/